DINOSAURS

Photo credits:
Francois Gohier—Pages 6, 7, 8, 9, 10, 11, 12, 13, 20, 22, 31
Dr. E.R. Degginger—Cover
Michael Rothman/Wildlife Collection—Page 14
AP/Wide World—Pages 16, 23, 30
Jan Sovak—Pages 17, 26, 27
Howard Friedman—Page 19
Phil Degginger— Page 28

ISBN: 0-590-96961-7

12 11 10 9 8 7 6 5 4 3 2 1   5 6 7 8 9/9 0/0

Printed in the U.S.A.   24

First Scholastic printing, November 1996

DINOSAURS

By Tracy Christopher

Scholastic Inc.
New York   Toronto   London   Auckland   Sydney

What Is a Dinosaur?

Dinosaurs were reptiles—relatives of snakes, crocodiles, lizards, and turtles. They lived millions of years ago. Some were the largest land animals that ever lived on Earth. Now they are gone. They all died out, or became *extinct*.

How Do We Know About Dinosaurs?

We learn about dinosaurs from clues, like the bones, teeth, and other traces they left behind. These traces are called *fossils*.

Paleontologists (PAY-lee-on-TOL-o-jists) are people who study fossils. By putting together fossil skeletons, they can tell us what dinosaurs looked like and how they lived.

Which Dinosaur Is That?

So far, hundreds of kinds of dinosaurs have been discovered.

Albertosaurus

Parasaurolophus

Nodosaur

They came in many different sizes and shapes. Some walked on four legs, others walked on two. Some ate plants, others ate meat.

Triceratops

Diplodocus

Edmontosaurs

Brachyceratops

Apatosaurus tracks

Apatosaurus

That's Big!

Apatosaurus (ah-PAT-uh-sawr-us) was one of the biggest dinosaurs. It had a long neck, a huge body, and four sturdy legs. It left tracks about two feet deep and three feet wide. That's big enough for a person to sit in!

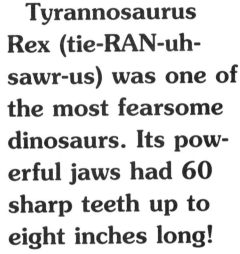

Tyrannosaurus Rex (tie-RAN-uh-sawr-us) was one of the most fearsome dinosaurs. Its powerful jaws had 60 sharp teeth up to eight inches long!

Tyrannosaurus skull

Small Dinosaurs

Not all dinosaurs were huge. Tiny Saltopus (SALT-o-pus) was about the size of a house cat.

Protoceratops

Coelophysis (seal-o-FIE-sis) had a head smaller than a human hand. At almost three feet tall, Protoceratops (pro-toe-SAIR-uh-tops) was about as tall as a three-year-old child.

Coelophysis skull

Dinosaur Life

Dinosaur fossils have been found throughout the world. Dinosaurs lived long ago in swamps, forests, and open plains.

Some dinosaurs lived in large groups, or herds. Others may have hunted in packs.

Out of Eggs

Almost all dinosaurs laid eggs. Some eggs found so far are about 10 times bigger than a chicken egg.

The first baby dinosaurs found in a nest were Maiasaura (mah-ee-ah-SAWR-uh). An adult Maiasaura lay nearby. This means that dinosaurs probably looked after their young.

Footprints show that a traveling herd of dinosaurs kept their young in the center for protection.

Brachiosaurus

Plant Eaters

The biggest dinosaurs were *herbivores*, or plant eaters. Trachodon (TRAK-uh-don) and other duck-billed dinosaurs were built for chewing plants. Their mouths were full of teeth—over 2,000 of them.

Other plant eaters, like Brachiosaurus (BRAK-ee-uh-sawr-us), used its long neck to reach leaves at the tops of trees.

Trachodon

Meat Eaters

    Carnivores, or meat eaters like Tyrannosaurus Rex, ran on two powerful hind legs. Their teeth were like steak knives with jagged edges.

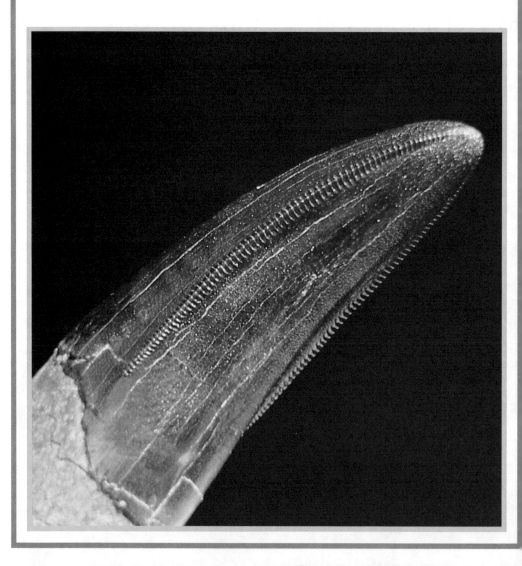

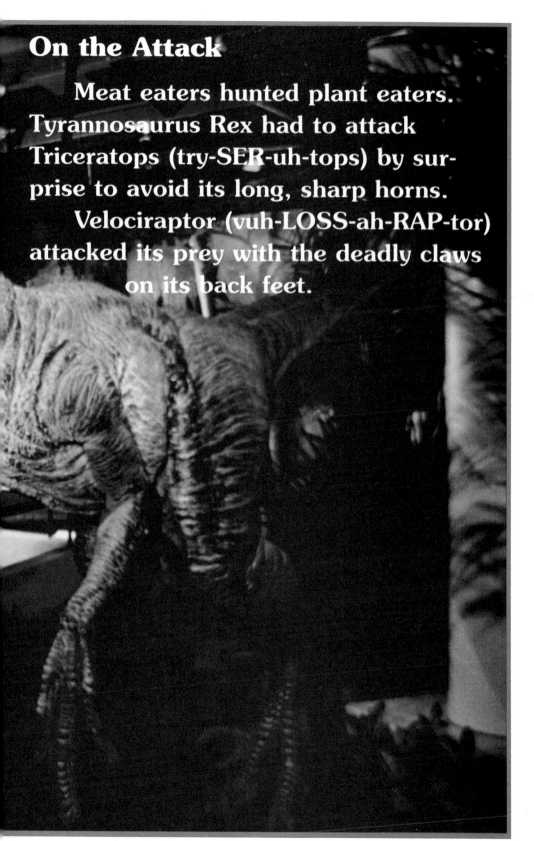

On the Attack

Meat eaters hunted plant eaters. Tyrannosaurus Rex had to attack Triceratops (try-SER-uh-tops) by surprise to avoid its long, sharp horns.

Velociraptor (vuh-LOSS-ah-RAP-tor) attacked its prey with the deadly claws on its back feet.

Defense!

Some plant eaters had armor for protection. Thick skin, bony plates, and a spiked tail protected Stegosaurus (steg-uh-SAWR-us) from its meat-eating enemies.

Styracosaurus (stih-RACK-uh-sawr-us) was protected from attack, too. It had horns and a bony frill around its neck!

The End of Dinosaurs

No one is sure why dinosaurs died out. Some scientists think that an asteroid, or giant rock from outer space, crashed into the earth. This crash raised enough dust into the air to block out sunlight for a long time. Plants died out. Then the plant-eating and meat-eating dinosaurs died, too.

Another theory is that there was a steep drop in temperature. The sudden cold weather killed all the dinosaurs.

Dinosaurs Today

You can see dinosaur skeletons in museums. Dinosaur bones have been discovered all over the world.

Scientists believe that there are hundreds, maybe even thousands more, waiting to be discovered.

Carcharodontosaurus skull

Did You Know?

• • The word "dinosaur" comes from Greek words for "terrible lizards."

• • Sometimes scientists find many dinosaur bones in one place. These "bone beds" may contain the bones of thousands of dinosaurs.

• • Paleontologist Paul Sereno recently discovered the skull of Carcharodontosaurus (car-CHAR-o-DONT-o-SAWR-us), the largest known skull of a meat-eating dinosaur. It is even larger than the head of Tyrannosaurus Rex!

Bone bed